Frédéric Le Bordays

COCKTAILS
THE NEW
CLASSICS

Photographer : Virginie Garnier
Stylist : Coralie Ferreira

weldon**owen**

I met Frédéric Le Bordays in Deauville, Lower Normandy. It was January of 2011, during a culinary festival. He proffered his services for cocktails—nonalcoholic ones. He had the look of a Prohibition-era New York bartender: custom-made shirt, retro black vest, old-school cap, and at least three days' beard. At the time, I was arranging a photography show about the Parisian cocktail scene, and I was looking for new rising stars. I'd heard about him: a very promising barman, at the very moment when a new era of French mixology was dawning in Paris.

A few months later, I found him again in order to take his portrait for a magazine. The article highlighted several tidbits from his recipe notebook and his passion for the world of vintage cocktails. I was still a booze neophyte, and that day, Frédéric became my mentor. He was steeped in the history of the golden age of cocktails and in the stories of the greatest barmen, from Jerry Thomas to Harry Craddock. An artist of the cocktail shaker and the bar spoon, he displayed a special ability and finesse in sharing his keen appreciation for old-fashioned digestifs and the elixirs dreamt up in the most prestigious American bars of the nineteenth century. From the Moscow mule to the Manhattan, from the most divinely sweet to the bone-driest dry, I tell you this: Frédéric had a true gift for electrifying the taste buds.

After exercising his talent in different Parisian hot spots, Frédéric continued on his own path, guided by his passion, putting together Mixed Drinks, a pop-up event that specialized in revisiting mythic cocktails. Drinks of the highest order, with service to match, attentive to the tiniest detail. Frédéric was one of the first French barmen to have the audacity and the foresight to bring vintage spirits and the great American tradition of classic cocktails back into style—an ambitious and daring gamble, faced as he was with a French audience that is more drawn to wine than to spirits.

This volume is the perfect reflection of Frédéric's expertise in cocktail lore, ranging from before Prohibition to our times, and of the richness of his experiments in mixology. I invite you to experience this book like a journey in time, and, of course, do not hesitate to test all of his recipes. Trust me: you are in good hands.

Laurence Marot
Mixology Journalist

Recalling certain gentlemen of other days, who made drinking one of the pleasures of life—not one of its evils ; and who, whatever they drank, proved able to carry it, keep their heads and remain gentlemen.

These lines, taken from the famed cocktail book *The Old Waldorf-Astoria Bar Book* (1935), nicely illustrate the state of the modern cocktail mindset of the last few years: advocating a return to responsible consumption based on quality, not quantity—in pursuit of sipping pleasure and not careless drunkenness.

Like the world of gastronomy, the cocktail world is undergoing a little revolution—or, shall we say, a return to its origins. We are rediscovering the artisanship of the bar and the barman's trade, its expert techniques, and the richness of its heritage. My gratitude goes to those passionate individuals who resuscitated the first cocktail books, dating from the second half of the nineteenth century, which gave rise to the Manhattan, the whiskey sour, and the gin fizz. It's during that era, considered the golden age of the cocktail, that the foundations of modern mixology were established.

No one can deny that cocktail culture profits from the current mania for all things vintage. Nevertheless, it is rewarding to notice that this popularity goes hand in hand with a certain attention to quality and a demand for constant progress. Excellence is no longer measured by the awarding of five stars; cocktails are democratic, and everyone can discover the pleasure of tasting one created according to the rules of the art.

This volume brings together a number of these forgotten cocktails, as well as historical information and techniques for creating them at home, but also more contemporary recipes that marry tradition with modernity.

———————————— Happy tasting! ————————————

A STIMULATING LIQUEUR

The origin of the word "cocktail" is uncertain, and one finds little documentation on the subject. Many theories have been put forward to explain the cocktail's appearance. One tends to hear about a Creole

apothecary, Antoine Amédée Peychaud, who set himself up in New Orleans at the beginning of the nineteenth century and who concocted a blend of cognac, absinthe, sugar, and aromatic bitters that he sold under the name "Peychaud's Bitters." He served this beverage, called "Sazerac" after the brand of cognac used, in an egg cup—or, as it is called in French creole, a *coquetier;* the mangling of this word by non–Creole speakers gave birth to the word "cocktail."

As for the origin of many recipes, it is difficult to determine the paternity of a mixture and—just between you and me—not very interesting. What's more, it seems to me difficult or even delusional to claim that a certain fellow was the first to mix whiskey with lemon juice and sugar without someone else at the other end of the earth having done the same thing . . . For this reason, it's important to take many claims and origin stories with a grain of salt and to concentrate on the written evidence.

One of the earliest references to the word "cocktail" appears in the journal *The Balance, and Columbian Repository* dated May 6, 1806. There, "cock tail" is defined as "a stimulating liqueur, composed of spirits of any kind, sugar, water, and bitters, vulgarly called a bitter sling."

It's interesting to note that the word "cocktail" has become the generic term for a mixture of drinks, while in the nineteenth century, it designated a very particular category of drinks, composed of a liquor, sugar, and aromatic bitters.

PUNCH, THE COCKTAIL ANCESTOR

The history of the cocktail and its evolution are intimately tied to great political and cultural movements. The British colonial empire certainly played a decisive role in the development of the cocktail in Europe and the United States, notably in its most popular form of the time: punch. The word "punch" resonates with the Hindi word *"panch,"* which means "five," a reference to the number of ingredients: spirits, lemon juice, sugar, water, and tea or spice. This preparation, brought back from India to England by sailors working for the British East India Tea Company at the beginning of the seventeenth century,

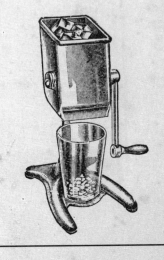

marks the birth of the cocktail as we know it today. It is prepared in nonreactive punch bowls, and generally includes brandy, rum, or gin. The advent of the gin & tonic, consumed to ward off malaria, also dates from this period.

★ ★ ★ ★ ★ ★ ★ ★
THE BOOKS
★ ★ ★ ★ ★ ★ ★ ★

It's on the other side of the Atlantic that we find the first works compiling popular recipes of the day. Jerry Thomas, considered the father of the modern cocktail, published *The Bar-Tender's Guide or How to Mix Drinks* in 1862. This early volume already offered recipes for the Manhattan cocktail, the gin fizz, and the whiskey sour, as well as details on methods of preparation and conservation. One could also cite Harry Johnson's *New and Improved Bartenders' Manual* in 1882, a veritable bible in which one finds complete information on how to run a tavern and manage staff, as well as, of course, numerous cocktail recipes.

PROHIBITION TIMES

Starting at the end of the nineteenth century, certain states began to limit the sale of alcoholic beverages. In 1919, the nineteenth amendment to the Constitution of the United States forbid the production and consumption of alcohol at a national level. This time period, known as Prohibition, marked a turning point in the history of the cocktail. Many distilleries disappeared, tolling the death knell of products like rye whiskey and aromatic bitters. Underground distilleries sprang up and fell into the hands of mafiosi, who cared little about the quality of their moonshine, which in turn spread death and intoxication in its wake. Clandestine bars, called "speakeasies" or "blind tigers," made their appearance.

Deprived of their business, bar professionals emigrated from the United States to Europe, and this contributed to the development of the cocktail on the Old Continent, notably in London and Paris. Harry's New York Bar in Paris and the Savoy Bar in London became cocktail meccas, with clienteles drinking white ladies and bloody Marys.

When Prohibition reached its high-water mark in the United States, they were drinking daiquiris and mojitos in Havana!

A RETURN TO THE SOURCE

We must wait until the end of the 1930s to see the cocktail make its return to American soil, notably thanks to the tiki craze (see page 55) that began to develop with the opening of Polynesian-influenced restaurants, like Don the Beachcomber in Hollywood and Trader Vic's in Palo Alto. They served fruity, rum-based cocktails in ceramic mugs depicting Polynesian totems.

And, it's not until the end of the 1990s that cocktails fully rediscovered their noble heritage, achieving a quality offering based on a balance of flavors rather than a mixture of colorful, sweet liqueurs aimed only at increasing the alcoholic content with drunkenness as the main goal. At last we can once again take pleasure in sipping cocktails prepared according to the rules of the art.

Cocktail Strainer

Ice Pick

Fine Strainer

EQUIPMENT

Bar spoon

The bar spoon harkens back to the nineteenth century, when apothecaries would use this style of spoon to crush tablets into water. Its long handle would let you reach the bottom of a glass and crush a pill against it. Thanks to a bowl that is a little deeper than that of a teaspoon, it could also be used to dose a patient with a syrup or another medicinal preparation.

Nowadays, its uses are:

✦ Measuring liquids—about a teaspoon when filled to the brim.

✦ Crushing sugar, fruits, or mint leaves, especially when outfitted with a hammer atop the handle.

✦ Mixing ingredients.

✦ Gently pouring and layering liquids, thanks to its twisted handle.

Cocktail strainer

This lets you keep the ice and solid ingredients inside a cocktail shaker when you're pouring the concoction into a cocktail glass.

Fine strainer

You can use a fine strainer along with a cocktail strainer to filter out the pesky little remnants left behind during cocktail preparation (bits of mint, citrus pulp...).

Ice pick

Used to chip ice.

Jigger

A jigger is used to measure out liquids. It's formed of two cups fused together in an hourglass shape, with the larger cup typically measuring 1 jigger, or shot, 1½ ounces (40 ml), and the smaller cup measuring ½ jigger, ¾ ounce (20 ml), or 1 pony, 1 ounce (25 ml). Many jiggers vary in size and can include other increments for measuring. A glass kitchen measuring cup or kitchen shot can also help with measuring small quantities of liquid.

Julep strainer

Back in the days when visiting the dentist was not such a popular pastime, you could use this strainer to prevent ice from getting into painful contact with your teeth. Nowadays we use it to keep the ice in a mixing glass when pouring out a cocktail.

Lemon juicer

A juicer is the quickest route to fresh citrus juice without pulp. Juicers come in a variety of different shapes and sizes, often color-coded according to the fruit you're planning to press.

Mixing glass

This preparation glass allows for mixing and chilling ingredients for a "stirred" cocktail. It needs to hold a volume of at least 2 cups (16 oz/500 ml). Look for a model with a pinched lip for pouring.

Muddler

Made of wood or plastic, a muddler is used to grind and crush aromatics, fruits, and ice. Plastic ones are easier to maintain compared to wood.

Shaker

The shaker fulfills a double function of mixing and chilling. It's used when ingredients with different consistencies or densities need to come together to create a cocktail (fruit juice, syrup, cream, egg...). There are three types of shakers:

✦ The Boston shaker has a lower part made of glass, in which the cocktail is prepared, and a top of stainless steel that fits together with the bottom. When the shaking commences, the stainless steel part contracts around the glass and creates an airtight seal. A strainer is used to keep the ice in the shaker when pouring the cocktail into a glass.

✦ The Continental shaker is identical to the Boston, but composed completely of stainless steel, which allows for better conduction of the coldness.

✦ The three-piece cobbler shaker offers the advantage of not having to use a strainer, as the top includes its own built-in strainer.

Coupette glass

Julep cup

Martini glass

Cocktail glass

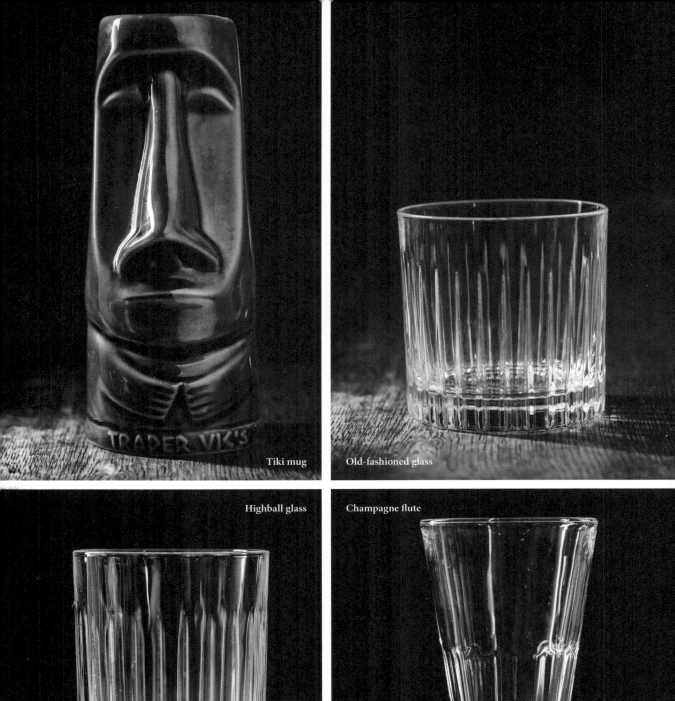

Tiki mug

Old-fashioned glass

Highball glass

Champagne flute

Chill the glass

TECHNIQUES

1. CHILL THE GLASSES

This is the first step. You can place the glasses in the freezer or fill them with ice before starting to mix the cocktail in order to keep it chilled longer. On the other hand, if you are serving a hot drink, pour hot water into the mug intended to hold it in order to bring it to a good temperature.

2. MEASURE THE INGREDIENTS

Measure out all the ingredients that make up the cocktail. If you proceed this way, you can modify and adjust your recipes in order to adapt them to your own taste. What's more, ingredients that are very concentrated or have a very intense flavor (chile infusions, very bitter bitters, very peaty whiskey …) must be precisely measured to keep the cocktail balanced.

3. PREPARE THE COCKTAIL

…with a shaker (shaken cocktail)

A shaker is recommended when the ingredients going into a cocktail are difficult to mix or have different consistencies: juice, syrup, egg, cream. Shaking a cocktail with ice obviously chills the concoction, but it also emulsifies the ingredients properly while bringing an airy consistency to the blend.

1. Pour all the ingredients into the bottom half of the shaker, then add the ice last, just before shaking, so that it doesn't melt and water down the mixture.

2. Put the top on and shake vigorously for at least 10 seconds.

3. Remove the lid and strain the cocktail into the serving glass. Always bear in mind:

✦ No more than two cocktails per shaker.

✦ Always fill the shaker three-quarters full of ice.

✦ Never reuse the ice.

✦ It's sometimes difficult to remove the top of the shaker. If you can't get it open, run it under hot water.

…in a mixing glass (stirred cocktail)

This technique is used to mix and chill cocktails composed only of spirits, liqueurs, or vermouths. It's a less brutal method and gives a silkier texture to the cocktail.

1. Pour all the ingredients into a mixing glass or the bottom half of a cocktail shaker.

2. Add the ice and stir with a bar

Measure the ingredients

Prepare the cocktail with a shaker

Prepare the cocktail in a mixing glass

spoon. This technique requires a little practice. You want to glide the back of the spoon along the wall of the mixing glass in a circular fashion for 15 to 20 seconds.

3. Use a julep strainer or cocktail strainer to keep the ice in the glass, and pour the concoction into the chilled serving glass.

... directly in the glass

Certain cocktails are prepared directly in the serving glass, often with the help of a bar spoon.

1. Fill the glass with ice.

2. Pour in the ingredients (starting with noncarbonated liquids).

3. Top with ice if needed, stir with the spoon, and serve.

... with a blender

A blender lets you mix frozen drinks, with granita-like textures.

... in a punch bowl

You can pour all the ingredients for a punch directly into a punch bowl made of glass, ceramic, stainless steel, or silver, and add ice cubes to chill the mixture— or, better yet, a block of ice, to delay diluting the mixture. You can also avoid the issue of melting ice by preparing the mixture in advance, then serving it directly in glasses, with just enough ice to keep the drink chilled. The quantities of punches are given in proportions rather than measured out to allow you to tailor the amount to suit your container.

4. SQUEEZE THE ZEST

As a final touch, you will often squeeze a strip of citrus zest over a cocktail to extract its flavorful and aromatic essential oils. Use a vegetable peeler to remove a 1- or 2-inch (2.5- or 5-mm) strip of zest, then squeeze it, with the colorful side facing the glass. You can flambé the oils of orange zest with a match or lighter by squeezing it next to the flame.

Strain the cocktail

Squeeze some zest

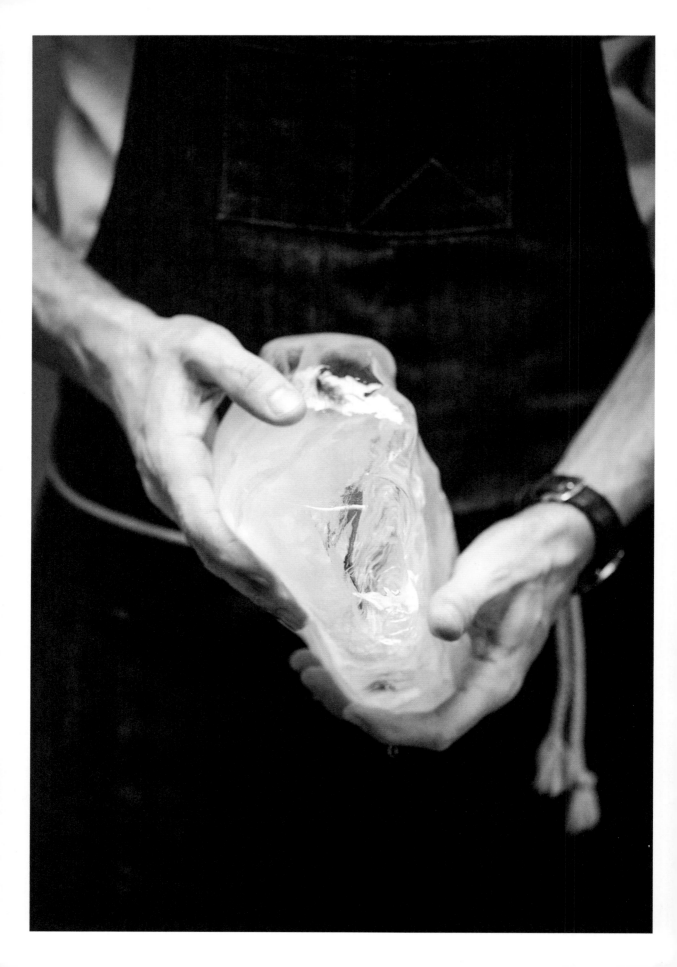

Large ice cube

Small ice cubes

Crushed ice

INGREDIENTS

ICE

Too often neglected, ice is in fact a key element in the preparation and tasting of a cocktail. It fulfills the dual roles of chilling and of correctly diluting. Good-quality ice will be very cold, dry, and quite transparent. The water used to make it should be filtered and as neutral as possible.

In the days when our cocktail pioneer forebearers exercised their talents, ice was delivered in the form of large blocks, and shards of different shapes and sizes were broken off with the help of a saw or ice pick.

To get good-quality ice at home, use mineral water or filtered tap water. Pour it into flexible molds at least 1 inch (2.5 cm) wide. These days there are silicone ice molds available that make ice cubes of various shapes and sizes. Another method is to freeze water in a Tupperware-type container and use an ice pick to chip it into large ice cubes about 5 inches (13 cm) wide.

To make crushed ice, wrap a few cubes in a clean dish towel and crush them with a heavy object or a mallet.

CITRUS JUICE

Along with ice, lemon juice is another commonly used ingredient, and its freshness, like that of other citrus juices, is essential. Use only freshly squeezed citrus juice that you've extracted yourself with a handheld juicer. You can keep it refrigerated for several hours.

SUGAR & SYRUPS

Sugar is used in a lot of recipes to balance out the acidity of citrus juice. Granulated sugar, even superfine, is hard to dissolve in cold liquids and in alcohol, and this is the reason for using liquid sugar.

+ Simple syrup is a mix of 1 part superfine sugar and 1 part mineral water, stirred over heat until the sugar dissolves.

+ Sugar syrup is a mix of 2 parts sugar and 1 part mineral water, stirred over heat until the sugar dissolves.

+ Gum syrup is a sugar syrup made with gum arabic, a resin from the acacia tree, incorporated into it. It brings a richer mouthfeel and weightier texture to cocktails.

It's very easy to make homemade syrups from fruits, spices, or aromatics by letting the flavoring agent macerate in sugar syrup for 24 hours.

AROMATIC PLANTS

Aromatics make the list of irreplaceable cocktail ingredients. Crushed or simply macerated in liquor or sugar syrup, aromatics are an inexhaustible source of inspiration and diverse flavors. Among those most often used are mint, basil, sage, lemongrass, and rosemary.

AROMATIC BITTERS

Bitters are flavor enhancers obtained by macerating and distilling aromatic plants, spices, or citrus peel in a base of alcohol. Very bitter, these preparations bring complexity and a lingering aftertaste to cocktails. They are an essential ingredient that you could call seasoning for a cocktail. Once taken as medicinal remedies, bitters earned their stripes in the nineteenth century. They were often used at that time in the preparation of mixed drinks. Many producers disappeared during Prohibition, but a renewed interest in nineteenth-century recipes has allowed certain vanished bitters brands, like Boker's and Abbott's, to come back on the market.

Aromatic bitters, unlike bitter German or Italian aperitifs like Campari, are not generally intended to be consumed on their own, but rather in combination with other ingredients. The best known and most used are Angostura bitters, Peychaud's bitters, and orange bitters.

VERMOUTHS

Vermouths are fortified white wine–based aperitifs flavored with plants such as cinchona bark. Traditionally, sweet vermouths come from Italy and dry vermouths from France, although one finds a complete gamut of vermouths made by each producer, such as Noilly-Prat, Martini & Rossi, Dolin, and Carpano. Sweet vermouths have an amber color and dry vermouths, a more clear appearance and very little sugar.

LIQUORS

Technically, a liquor (or spirit) is the product of distilling a lightly alcoholic liquid created from fruits, grains, or other plants. This includes vodka, whiskey, cognac, gin … we won't belabor the production details of each type here—that could be the topic of an entire separate volume—but you will find notes in this book's recipes explaining the origin and details of production of some of these liquors.

To put together a good cocktail, high-quality ingredients are imperative: a few dollars more can truly make a difference, so please use the top-shelf brands!

LIQUEURS

Liqueurs are made from distilled spirits and flavors from fruits or other plants. They generally contain less alcohol and more added sugar than liquors. Certain liqueurs that were very popular during the golden age of cocktails have lately come back on the scene: Bénédictine, Chartreuse, maraschino liqueur, and triple sec were always on hand at classic bars.

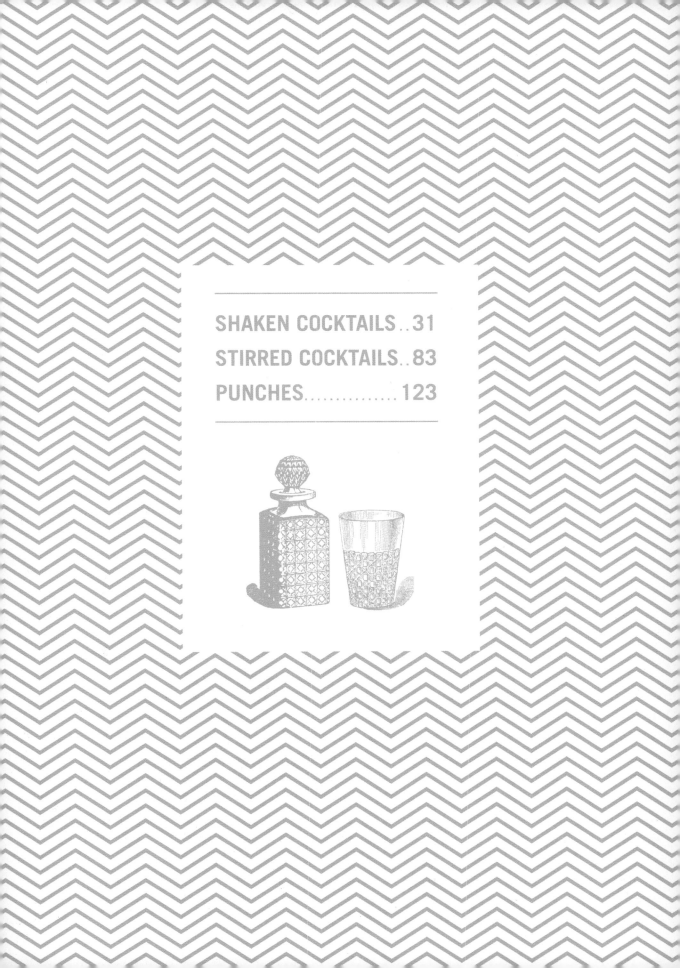

Shaken Cocktails

AVIATION COCKTAIL

Hugo Ensslin, chief barman of the Wallick Hotel in New York at the beginning of the twentieth century, was the first to present this recipe, in 1916, in his book Recipes for Mixed Drinks. *Works that followed this early publication, including the 1930s reference to the* Savoy Cocktail Book, *almost always omitted the violet liqueur. It appears that difficulty in procuring violet liqueur—then and now—has led certain barmen to omit it from the preparation.*

* 2 OZ (60 ML) GIN
* ¾ OZ (20 ML) LEMON JUICE
* ½ OZ (15 ML) MARASCHINO LIQUEUR
* 2 TSP (10 ML) CRÈME DE VIOLETTE (VIOLET LIQUEUR)

Pour all the ingredients into a shaker, add ice, and shake vigorously.

Strain into a chilled cocktail glass.

GARNISH : squeeze a strip of lemon zest over the glass, and garnish with a cherry.

BLACK & TAN

The origin of the black & tan is uncertain. It is supposed to have been created at the end of the nineteenth century at the Country Club in Baltimore; however, the use of ginger beer in cocktails did not become widespread until the 1950s, which casts some doubt on this theory.

⋆ 8 MINT LEAVES
⋆ 2 TSP (10 ML) LIME JUICE
⋆ 2 TSP (10 ML) SIMPLE SYRUP
⋆ 5 BLACKBERRIES
⋆ 2 OZ (60 ML) RYE WHISKEY
⋆ GINGER BEER

In a shaker, lightly muddle the mint with the lime juice and syrup.

Add the blackberries and the rye. Fill the shaker with ice and shake vigorously.

Strain into an ice-filled highball glass and top off with ginger beer.

GARNISH : spear 2 blackberries on a cocktail pick.

RYE WHISKEY

Very popular in the United States before Prohibition, rye is the result of a distillation of rye grain (at least 51 percent), aged in fire-charred oak barrels. Rye appears in many nineteenth-century recipes, such as the Manhattan and the Sazerac.

BLOOD & SAND

We find the first mention of the blood & sand in the famous Savoy Cocktail Book, put together in 1930 by Harry Craddock and now considered a classic drink reference. This is one of the few cocktails featuring Scotch.

⭑ 1 OZ (25 ML) SCOTCH WHISKY
⭑ 1 OZ (25 ML) SWEET VERMOUTH
⭑ 1 OZ (25 ML) CHERRY LIQUEUR
⭑ 1 OZ (25 ML) ORANGE JUICE

Pour all the ingredients into a shaker, add ice, and shake vigorously.

Strain into a chilled cocktail glass.

GARNISH : squeeze a strip of orange zest over the glass, and drop it in.

BRANDY CRUSTA

Published for the first time in the 1862 edition of Jerry Thomas's work The Bar-Tender's Guide, *the brandy crusta recipe was supposedly created by Joseph Santina, proprietor of City Exchange Bar in New Orleans, in 1852.*

* 1 LEMON
* SUPERFINE SUGAR
* 2 OZ (60 ML) COGNAC
* ½ OZ (15 ML) CURAÇAO
* ½ OZ (15 ML) LEMON JUICE
* 2 TSP (10 ML) SUGAR SYRUP
* 2 DASHES BOKER'S BITTERS OR ANGOSTURA BITTERS

Zest the lemon as you would peel an apple, then cut in half. Prepare a little cocktail glass by rubbing the rim with the cut lemon half, then dipping it into superfine sugar spread on a saucer. Place the lemon zest inside the glass.

Pour all the remaining ingredients into a shaker, add ice, and shake vigorously, then strain into the prepared cocktail glass.

CHAMPS-ÉLYSÉES COCKTAIL

Harry Craddock documented this cocktail homage to the Parisian granddaddy of all boulevards in his 1930 Savoy Cocktail Book.

✶ 2 OZ (60 ML) COGNAC
✶ ¾ OZ (20 ML) CHARTREUSE
✶ ¾ OZ (20 ML) LEMON JUICE
✶ 2 TSP (10 ML) SIMPLE SYRUP
✶ 1 DASH ANGOSTURA BITTERS

Pour all the ingredients into a shaker, add ice, and shake vigorously.

Strain into a chilled cocktail glass.

CHARTREUSE

Chartreuse is an herbal liqueur produced in Voiron, in the Isère department of southeastern France. Concocted of more than a hundred plants, it is available in several varieties, the best known being green Chartreuse and yellow Chartreuse.

In the Champs-Élysées cocktail, Harry Craddock doesn't specify which to use, but either of these liqueurs works just as well as the other.

CLOVER CLUB

From 1882 to 1920, the Clover Club was a little group of journalists who met once a month at the Bellevue-Stratford hotel in Philadelphia to eat, drink, and discuss. The group gave its name to a cocktail that was popular among its members. Use an artisanal raspberry syrup or, if you have the time to make your own, turn to page 26 for instructions. The egg white brings a smooth lightness to the preparation.

* 1½ OZ (40 ML) GIN
* 1 OZ (25 ML) LEMON JUICE
* ½ OZ (15 ML) RASPBERRY SYRUP
* 2 TSP SUPERFINE SUGAR
* 1 FRESH EGG WHITE

Pour all the ingredients into a shaker and shake without ice to blend the mixture (this is known as a dry shake).

Add ice and shake vigorously.

Strain into a chilled cocktail glass.

GARNISH : spear 1 raspberry on a cocktail pick.

CORPSE REVIVER N°2

CORPSE REVIVER Nº2

We find the first mention of the corpse reviver recipe in the Savoy Cocktail Book, *assembled in 1930 by Harry Craddock. "Corpse revivers" are part of a family of cocktails with supposed curative properties, or more precisely, hangover remedies. In his volume, Harry Craddock says of the corpse reviver no2: "Four of these taken in swift succession will unrevive the corpse again."*

* 1 OZ (25 ML) DRY GIN
* 1 OZ (25 ML) TRIPLE SEC
* 1 OZ (25 ML) WHITE LILLET
* 1 OZ (25 ML) LEMON JUICE
* 1 DASH (ABOUT 1 TSP) ABSINTHE

Pour all the ingredients into a shaker, add ice, and shake vigorously.

Strain into a chilled cocktail glass.

GARNISH : squeeze a strip of lemon zest over the glass, and drop it in.

CORPSE REVIVER Nº1

Variation on Corpse Reviver Nº2 (stirred cocktail)

* 1½ OZ (40 ML) COGNAC
* ¾ OZ (20 ML) SWEET VERMOUTH
* ¾ OZ (20 ML) CALVADOS

Pour all the ingredients into a mixing glass, add ice, and stir with a bar spoon.

Strain into a chilled cocktail glass.

DAIQUIRI

Much like the caipirinha in Brazil, the daiquiri is the drink of the Cuban everyman. Popularized by Ernest Hemingway, today it is one of the best-known tropical cocktails, along with the mojito.

* 2 OZ (60 ML) CUBAN RUM
* ¾ OZ (20 ML) LIME JUICE
* 2 TSP (10 ML) SUGAR SYRUP

Pour all the ingredients into a shaker, add ice, and shake vigorously.

Strain into a chilled cocktail glass.

GARNISH : add 1 lime round or quarter.

DAIQUIRI

HEMINGWAY SPECIAL

HEMINGWAY SPECIAL

Variation on Daiquiri

Ernest Hemingway, who suffered from a rare form of diabetes, asked the chief barman of the Floridita, Constantino Ribalaigua Vert, to make him a daiquiri with two shots of rum and no sugar. This version was called a "papa doble," "Papa" being the nickname that the Cubans had given Hemingway. Years later, another Floridita barman, Antonio Meilán, added some maraschino liqueur and grapefruit juice to Constantino's recipe, and the papa doble became the Hemingway special.

* 2 OZ (60 ML) CUBAN RUM
* ½ OZ (15 ML) MARASCHINO LIQUEUR
* ½ OZ (15 ML) LIME JUICE
* ½ OZ (15 ML) GRAPEFRUIT JUICE
* 2 TSP (10 ML) SUGAR SYRUP

Pour all the ingredients into a shaker, add ice, and shake vigorously.

Strain into a chilled cocktail glass.

GARNISH : squeeze a strip of grapefruit zest over the glass, and drop it in.

NUCLEAR DAIQUIRI
Variation on Daiquiri

This modern classic was created in 2005 by Gregor de Gruyther, at the bar LAB in London's Soho district.

* 1 OZ (25 ML) WRAY & NEPHEW WHITE OVERPROOF RUM
* 1 OZ (25 ML) GREEN CHARTREUSE
* 1 OZ (25 ML) LIME JUICE
* 2 TSP (10 ML) VELVET FALERNUM

Pour all the ingredients into a shaker, add ice, and shake vigorously.

Strain into a chilled cocktail glass.

GARNISH : add 1 lime round.

WRAY & NEPHEW OVERPROOF RUM

Wray & Nephew overproof rum is a white rum distilled in Jamaica that clocks in at 62.8 percent alcohol. Its elevated alcohol level makes it mainly appropriate for cocktails. It's very popular in Jamaica, where it's mixed with Coca-Cola or ginger beer.

ESPRESSO MARTINI

This cocktail was created in London by the celebrated barman Dick Bradsell, at the end of the 1980s. Traditionally, Polish vodkas are made from rye and Russian vodkas from wheat. The quality of the coffee is obviously a factor in the success of this recipe.

* 2 OZ (60 ML) RYE-BASED VODKA
* ¾ OZ (20 ML) COFFEE LIQUEUR
* 1½ OZ (40 ML) ESPRESSO
* 1 TSP (5 ML) SUGAR SYRUP

Pour all the ingredients into a shaker, add ice, and shake vigorously.

Strain into a chilled cocktail glass.

GARNISH : float 3 coffee beans on the surface of the cocktail.

JALISCO ESPRESSO MARTINI

Variation on Espresso Martini (stirred cocktail)

* 2 OZ (60 ML) TEQUILA (100% AGAVE)
* 1 OZ (25 ML) COFFEE LIQUEUR
* 1½ OZ (40 ML) ESPRESSO

Pour all the ingredients into a mixing glass, add ice, and stir with a bar spoon.

Strain into a chilled cocktail glass.

GARNISH : float 3 coffee beans on the surface of the cocktail.

ESPRESSO MARTINI

IMPROVED RUM DAISY

I created this cocktail for Mixed Drinks Paris.

- ⚹ 2 OZ (60 ML) BARBADOS RHUM VIEUX (AGED RUM)
- ⚹ ½ OZ (15 ML) VELVET FALERNUM
- ⚹ 1 OZ (25 ML) LIME JUICE
- ⚹ 2 TSP (10 ML) ORGEAT SYRUP
- ⚹ 1 DASH ABSINTHE
- ⚹ 1 DASH ANGOSTURA BITTERS
- ⚹ SPARKLING WATER
- ⚹ 1 DASH PEYCHAUD'S BITTERS

Pour all the ingredients except the sparkling water and Peychaud's bitters into a shaker, add ice, and shake vigorously.

Strain into a tiki mug or a highball glass full of crushed ice. Top off with sparkling water and Peychaud's bitters.

GARNISH : add 1 mint sprig and 1 strip lemon zest.

TIKI

Tiki culture, inspired by Polynesian culture, took off in the United States in the early 1930s. It was born on the West Coast, notably with the launch of restaurants like Don the Beachcomber and Trader Vic's, where they served rum-based cocktails in ceramic mugs representing Polynesian wooden sculptures.

Velvet Falernum is a Caribbean liqueur flavored with ginger, clove, and lime, often used in tiki cocktails.

MAI TAI

The mai tai was created by Victor J. Bergeron (Trader Vic) in Oakland, California, in 1944. It became very popular in the 1950s and is today an integral part of tiki culture. "Mai tai" can be translated as "good" or "the best" in Tahitian. The rum used in the 1944 recipe, Wray & Nephew 17 year, is no longer produced.

★ 2 OZ (60 ML) JAMAICAN AMBER RUM
★ ½ OZ (15 ML) CURAÇAO
★ ½ OZ (15 ML) ORGEAT SYRUP
★ JUICE OF 1 LIME
★ 1 TSP (5 ML) SUGAR SYRUP MADE FROM RAW SUGAR

Pour all the ingredients into a shaker, add ice, and shake vigorously.

Strain into an ice-filled old-fashioned glass.

GARNISH : add 1 mint sprig.

CURAÇAO

Curaçao is an orange-flavored liqueur invented by the Dutch and traditionally based on brandy, while triple sec (Cointreau, for example) is also an orange-flavored liqueur, but based on neutral alcohol. The most popular brand of curaçao is Grand Marnier Cordon Rouge.

MOLE MEXICANO

Here is another of my concoctions for Mixed Drinks Paris.

- ✶ 1 LIME, QUARTERED
- ✶ COCOA POWDER
- ✶ 1 OZ (25 ML) MEZCAL
- ✶ 1 OZ (25 ML) REPOSADO TEQUILA (100% AGAVE)
- ✶ ½ OZ (15 ML) DARK CRÈME DE CACAO (CHOCOLATE LIQUEUR)
- ✶ 1 OZ (25 ML) LIME JUICE
- ✶ 2 TSP (10 ML) CHILE-INFUSED AGAVE NECTAR (SEE OPPOSITE)
- ✶ 2 DASHES CHOCOLATE BITTERS

Prepare a cocktail glass by rubbing the rim with a lime quarter, then dipping it into cocoa powder spread on a saucer.

Pour all the remaining ingredients into a shaker, add ice, and shake vigorously.

Strain into the prepared cocktail glass.

CHILE-INFUSED AGAVE NECTAR

To infuse agave nectar with chiles,
halve 5 little red chiles lengthwise
and let them macerate in 2 cups
(16 oz/500 ml) agave nectar overnight,
then pour through a fine strainer.

PENICILLIN

In 2005, Sam Ross created this cocktail for New York's Milk & Honey bar. In the spirit of an apothecary's original, it will cure what ails you.

★ 1¾ OZ (50 ML) SCOTCH WHISKY
★ 1 OZ (25 ML) LEMON JUICE
★ 1 OZ (25 ML) HONEY SYRUP
★ 1 TSP (5 ML) FRESH GINGER JUICE
★ 2 TSP (10 ML) ISLAY WHISKY

Pour all the ingredients except the Islay whisky into a shaker, add ice, and shake vigorously.

Strain into an ice-filled old-fashioned glass, and carefully pour the Islay whisky over the back of a bar spoon so that it floats on top.

GARNISH : add 1 slice fresh ginger.

RAMOS GIN FIZZ

This zesty concoction was invented in 1888 by Henry Carl Ramos at the Imperial Cabinet Saloon, in New Orleans. At the time of its creation, the Ramos gin fizz was shaken for such a long time, at least a dozen minutes, that it had to be passed from hand to hand among a number of barmen before being served. This entertaining spectacle of hard-working "shaker boys" contributed to the commercial success of Mr. Henry C. Ramos.

* 1¾ OZ (50 ML) GIN
* 1 OZ (25 ML) HEAVY CREAM
* ¾ OZ (20 ML) SUGAR SYRUP
* ½ OZ (15 ML) LEMON JUICE
* ½ OZ (15 ML) LIME JUICE
* 1 FRESH EGG WHITE
* 1 TSP (5 ML) ORANGE FLOWER WATER
* SPARKLING WATER

Pour all the ingredients except the sparkling water into a shaker and shake without ice to blend the mixture (this is known as a dry shake). You can also use a blender, without ice.

Add ice to the shaker and shake vigorously for at least 1 minute. Strain into a chilled highball glass. Top off with sparkling water.

GARNISH : add 1 mint sprig.

WHISKEY SMASH

Along with juleps, smashes were very popular in the mid-nineteenth century in the United States. With their base of fresh mint, sugar, and liquor, smashes were prepared with a three-piece shaker, while juleps were mixed directly in the glass. The lemon was added in later years.

* 6 MINT LEAVES
* ½ LEMON, QUARTERED
* 2 OZ (60 ML) RYE WHISKEY OR BOURBON
* ¾ OZ (20 ML) SUGAR SYRUP

In a shaker, muddle the mint with the lemon pieces.

Add the remaining ingredients and ice, then shake.

Pour through a fine strainer into an ice-filled old-fashioned glass.

GARNISH : add 1 mint sprig.

SHISO GIN SMASH

Variation on Whiskey Smash

Here is my modern take on a smash, created for Mixed Drinks Paris.

* 3 GREEN SHISO LEAVES
* 1 OZ (25 ML) LIME JUICE
* 2 OZ (60 ML) GIN
* ¾ OZ (20 ML) SIMPLE SYRUP
* 2 DASHES CARDAMOM BITTERS

In a shaker, muddle the green shiso with the lime juice.

Add the remaining ingredients and ice, then shake.

Pour through a fine strainer into an ice-filled old-fashioned glass.

GARNISH : add 1 green shiso leaf.

SHISO GIN SMASH

THE BRAMBLE

This modern classic cocktail strikes a perfect balance between sourness from the lemon juice, sweetness from the sugar syrup, and fruitiness from the blackberry liqueur. It was created in London by Dick Bradsell.

* 1¾ OZ (50 ML) GIN
* 1 OZ (25 ML) LEMON JUICE
* 2 TSP (10 ML) SUGAR SYRUP
* ½ OZ (15 ML) CRÈME DE MÛRE (BLACKBERRY LIQUEUR)

Pour all the ingredients except the crème de mûre into a shaker, add ice, and shake vigorously.

Strain into an ice-filled old-fashioned glass, and carefully pour the crème de mûre over the back of a bar spoon so that it floats on top.

GARNISH : add 1 lemon slice and 1 blackberry.

THE LAST WORD

The last word is supposed to have been uttered in the 1920s, at the Detroit Athletic Club, an august private establishment.

★ 1 OZ (25 ML) GIN
★ 1 OZ (25 ML) GREEN CHARTREUSE
★ 1 OZ (25 ML) MARASCHINO LIQUEUR
★ 1 OZ (25 ML) LIME JUICE

Pour all the ingredients into a shaker, add ice, and shake vigorously.

Strain into a chilled cocktail glass.

THE LAPHROAIG PROJECT
Variation on The Last Word

Owen Westman created this cocktail at Bourbon & Branch, San Francisco, a Prohibition era–styled speakeasy that requires a password for entrance.

★ 1 OZ (25 ML) GREEN CHARTREUSE
★ 1 OZ (25 ML) LEMON JUICE
★ ½ OZ (15 ML) LAPHROAIG QUARTER CASK WHISKY
★ ½ OZ (15 ML) MARASCHINO LIQUEUR
★ 1½ TSP (7 ML) YELLOW CHARTREUSE
★ 2 DASHES PEACH BITTERS

Pour all the ingredients into a shaker, add ice, and shake vigorously.

Strain into an ice-filled old-fashioned glass.

GARNISH : squeeze a strip of lemon zest over the glass, and drop it in.

TOMMY'S MARGARITA

This refined version of the classic, replacing triple sec with agave nectar, was created by Julio Bermejo of Tommy's Mexican Restaurant, in San Francisco.

⚹ 2 OZ (60 ML) TEQUILA (100% AGAVE)
⚹ 1 OZ (25 ML) LIME JUICE
⚹ ½ OZ (15 ML) AGAVE NECTAR

Pour all the ingredients into a shaker, add ice, and shake vigorously.

Strain into an ice-filled old-fashioned glass.

GARNISH : add an optional salt rim to the glass by rubbing it with a cut lime half and dipping it in salt spread on a saucer.

TEQUILA

Tequila is a liquor produced by the distillation of a type of agave. There are two categories of tequila: the 100-percent-agave ones and the lesser-quality *mixtos* (at least 60 percent agave). The 100-percent-agave tequilas are covered by a protected designation of origin and may be produced only in the Mexican state of Jalisco as well as certain municipalities in the states of Nayarit, Michoacán, Tamaulipas, and Guanajuato. These tequilas can be aged in oak barrels to give roundness to the body and complexity to the flavor. Each tequila is the expression of the terroir where it is produced.

TWENTIETH CENTURY COCKTAIL

This drink was invented in 1937 by British barman C. A. Tuck in honor of the famous 20th Century Limited train that linked New York to Chicago from 1902 to 1967. The recipe was published in 1937 in William J. Tarling's Cafe Royal Cocktail Book. *Originally, the cocktail was made with Kina Lillet, precursor of today's white Lillet and part of the family of quinquinas, or kinas—aperitif wines containing cinchona bark, a source of quinine (a useful antimalarial). You can use white Lillet or another quinquina, such as Cocchi Americano or Kina l'Avion d'Or.*

★ 1½ OZ (40 ML) GIN

★ ¾ OZ (20 ML) LEMON JUICE

★ ¾ OZ (20 ML) WHITE LILLET

★ ¾ OZ (20 ML) CRÈME DE CACAO (CHOCOLATE LIQUEUR)

Pour all the ingredients into a shaker, add ice, and shake vigorously.

Strain into a chilled cocktail glass.

GARNISH : squeeze a strip of lemon zest over the glass, and drop it in.

WHISKEY SOUR

The term "sour" indicates a cocktail composed of a spirit (whiskey, gin, rum…), lemon juice, sugar, egg white, and aromatic bitters.

★ 1¾ OZ (50 ML) WHISKEY

★ 1 OZ (25 ML) LEMON JUICE

★ ¾ OZ (20 ML) SIMPLE SYRUP

★ 1 FRESH EGG WHITE

★ 2 DASHES ANGOSTURA BITTERS

Pour all the ingredients into a shaker and shake without ice to blend the mixture (this is known as a dry shake).

Add ice and shake vigorously.

Serve on the rocks, in an ice-filled old-fashioned glass, or neat, in a chilled cocktail glass.

GARNISH : squeeze a strip of orange zest over the glass, and drop it in.

WHITE LADY

Variation on Whiskey Sour

Harry MacElhone, the Scottish founder of Harry's New York Bar in Paris, created this elegant offering in 1923. It makes a wonderful brunch cocktail.

★ 2 OZ (60 ML) GIN

★ ¾ OZ (20 ML) TRIPLE SEC

★ ¾ OZ (20 ML) LEMON JUICE

★ 1 FRESH EGG WHITE

Pour all the ingredients into a shaker and shake without ice to blend the mixture (this is known as a dry shake).

Add ice and shake vigorously.

Strain into a chilled cocktail glass.

GARNISH : squeeze a strip of grapefruit zest over the glass, and drop it in.

PISCO SOUR
Variation on Whiskey Sour

---

* 1¾ OZ (50 ML) PISCO
* 1 OZ (25 ML) LEMON JUICE
* ¾ OZ (20 ML) SIMPLE SYRUP
* 1 FRESH EGG WHITE
* 3 DASHES AMARGO CHUNCHO BITTERS

Pour all the ingredients into a shaker, add ice, and shake vigorously.

Strain into an ice-filled old-fashioned glass.

GARNISH : squeeze a strip of lime zest over the glass, and drop it in.

SAVOY TANGO SOUR
Variation on Whiskey Sour

I sour-ized the classic Savoy tango cocktail in this creation for Mixed Drinks Paris. The gentian liqueur gives it an extra note of bitterness.

---

* 1 OZ (25 ML) CALVADOS
* 1 OZ (25 ML) SLOE GIN (BLACKTHORN PLUM LIQUEUR)
* 1 OZ (25 ML) LEMON JUICE
* ½ OZ (15 ML) SUGAR SYRUP
* 1 FRESH EGG WHITE
* 1 DASH GENTIAN LIQUEUR

Pour all the ingredients except the gentian into a shaker, add ice, and shake vigorously.

Pour the gentian into a chilled cocktail glass, swirl the glass to coat the sides with the liqueur, then pour out the excess. Strain the contents of the shaker into the gentian-rinsed glass.

GARNISH : add 1 slice apple.

WINTER SHERRY FLIP

Here's another of my creations for Mixed Drinks Paris. A "flip" is a drink prepared with a whole egg, a liquor or fortified wine (port, for example), sugar, and spices, all well shaken. The first mentions of this type of recipe date from the second half of the nineteenth century, notably in Jerry Thomas's cocktail recipe book The Bar-Tender's Guide, *where we find examples like the cold brandy flip and the cold sherry wine flip.*

★ 1 OZ (25 ML) PEDRO XIMÉNEZ SHERRY

★ 1 OZ (25 ML) COGNAC

★ 2 TSP (10 ML) SWEET VERMOUTH

★ ½ OZ (15 ML) HOMEMADE CINNAMON, ORANGE PEEL, AND CLOVE SYRUP (SEE PAGE 26)

★ ½ OZ (15 ML) HEAVY CREAM

★ 1 FRESH WHOLE EGG

Pour all the ingredients into a shaker, add ice, and shake vigorously.

Strain into a chilled highball glass.

GARNISH : grate coffee beans over the top.

SHERRY

Sherry is a Spanish fortified wine, meaning a wine whose fermentation is interrupted by the addition of alcohol, which increases the residual sugar. Pedro Ximénez is the name of the grape varietal used in sherry production, indicating a "true" sherry.

Stirred Cocktails

BIJOU COCKTAIL

Here we have a real gem taken from Harry Johnson's New and Improved Bartenders' Manual, originally assembled in 1882. This cocktail is called "bijou," French for "jewel," because the three ingredients that compose it bring to mind the colors of diamonds, rubies, and emeralds.

* 1 OZ (25 ML) GIN
* 1 OZ (25 ML) SWEET VERMOUTH
* 1 OZ (25 ML) GREEN CHARTREUSE
* 1 DASH ORANGE BITTERS

Pour all the ingredients into a mixing glass, add ice, and stir with a bar spoon.

Strain into a chilled cocktail glass.

GARNISH : squeeze a strip of lemon zest over the glass, and drop it in.

DRY MARTINI

Plenty has been said and written about how to make the perfect dry martini: whether it should be shaken or stirred, what might be the proper proportions of vermouth, gin, and orange bitters. The dry martini is a great playing field for amateur mixologists: please experiment with the quantities and suit your own taste!

⋆ 2 OZ (60 ML) GIN
⋆ 2 TSP (10 ML) DRY VERMOUTH
⋆ 2 DASHES ORANGE BITTERS

Pour all the ingredients into a mixing glass, add ice, and stir with a bar spoon.

Strain into a chilled cocktail glass.

GARNISH : squeeze a strip of lemon zest over the glass, and drop it in. Add a green olive.

VESPER

Variation on Dry Martini (shaken cocktail)

This variation on the dry martini is taken from Ian Fleming's novel Casino Royale, *published in 1951.*

⋆ 2 OZ (60 ML) GIN
⋆ ¾ OZ (20 ML) VODKA
⋆ 2 TSP (10 ML) WHITE LILLET

Pour all the ingredients into a shaker, add ice, and shake vigorously.

Strain into a chilled cocktail glass.

GARNISH : squeeze a strip of lemon zest over the glass, and drop it in.

DRY MARTINI

VESPER

FANCY CHAMPAGNE COBBLER

SHERRY COBBLER

Sherry cobblers were very popular at the beginning of the nineteenth century. They would make them with either champagne or Bordeaux wine.

* 3 OZ (80 ML) FINO SHERRY
* 1 ORANGE SLICE, QUARTERED
* 2 TSP SUGAR

Combine all the ingredients in a shaker, add ice, and shake vigorously.

Strain into an ice-filled old-fashioned glass.

GARNISH : add seasonal fruits.

FANCY CHAMPAGNE COBBLER

Variation on Sherry Cobbler

Here's another of my offerings at Mixed Drinks Paris.

* ½ OZ (15 ML) LEMON JUICE
* ½ OZ (15 ML) ELDERFLOWER LIQUEUR
* 2 TSP (10 ML) FINO SHERRY
* 1 DASH ORANGE BITTERS
* CHAMPAGNE
* 2 DASHES ANGOSTURA BITTERS

Pour the lemon juice, elderflower liqueur, sherry, and orange bitters into a wineglass. Stir with a bar spoon.

Fill the glass with crushed ice and top off with champagne.

Add more crushed ice as needed, and season with Angostura bitters to taste.

GARNISH : add 1 mint sprig and seasonal fruits.

HANKY PANKY

Ada Coleman, chief barwoman at the American Bar of the Savoy Hotel in London, didn't mess around. "Coley" was the most popular barwoman of the 1920s, the moment when cocktails were increasing in popularity across Europe. She created this cocktail for one of her regular clients.

* 1½ OZ (40 ML) SWEET VERMOUTH
* 1½ OZ (40 ML) GIN
* 1 TSP (5 ML) FERNET-BRANCA

Pour all the ingredients into a mixing glass, add ice, and stir with a bar spoon.

Strain into a chilled cocktail glass.

JAPANESE COCKTAIL

This recipe is drawn from Jerry Thomas's The Bar-Tender's Guide, *published in 1862.*

⚹ 2 OZ (60 ML) COGNAC
⚹ ½ OZ (15 ML) ORGEAT SYRUP
⚹ 2 DASHES BOKER'S BITTERS OR ANGOSTURA BITTERS

Pour all the ingredients into a mixing glass, add ice, and stir with a bar spoon.

Strain into a chilled cocktail glass.

GARNISH : squeeze a strip of lemon zest over the glass, and drop it in.

MANHATTAN COCKTAIL

Just like the martini, this great cocktail classic boasts too many versions and variations to even count. No one really knows when the holy trio of rye whiskey, sweet vermouth, and aromatic bitters was first conceived, but we already find this tidbit in the 1862 The Bar-Tender's Guide *by Jerry Thomas: a Manhattan cocktail, composed of "2 dashes curaçao or maraschino liqueur, 1 pony rye whiskey, 1 wine glass vermouth and 3 dashes Boker's bitters." All the subtlety of this cocktail, with its relatively simple composition, comes into play with the quality of its ingredients—and, of course, the know-how of the mixologist!*

★ 2 OZ (60 ML) RYE WHISKEY

★ 1 OZ (25 ML) SWEET VERMOUTH

★ 2 DASHES ANGOSTURA BITTERS

Pour all the ingredients into a mixing glass, add ice, and stir with a bar spoon.

Strain into a chilled cocktail glass.

GARNISH : squeeze a strip of orange zest over the glass, and garnish with 1 cherry.

REMEMBER THE MAINE
Variation on Manhattan Cocktail

This drink, named after the rallying cry of the Spanish-American War (1898), was recorded in the Gentleman's Companion *by Charles H. Baker, Jr.*

★ 2 OZ (60 ML) RYE WHISKEY
★ 1 OZ (25 ML) SWEET VERMOUTH
★ 1½ TSP (7 ML) CHERRY HEERING
★ 2 DASHES ANGOSTURA BITTERS
★ 1 DASH ABSINTHE

Pour all the ingredients except the absinthe into a mixing glass, add ice, and stir with a bar spoon.

Pour the absinthe into a chilled cocktail glass, swirl the glass to coat the sides with the liqueur, then pour out the excess. Strain the contents of the mixing glass into the absinthe-rinsed glass.

GARNISH : add a strip of lemon zest.

REMEMBER THE MAINE

GREEN POINT
Variation on Manhattan Cocktail

Michael McIlroy of New York's Milk & Honey added herbaceous Chartreuse for his meditation on the Manhattan, created in the 2000s.

★ 2 OZ (60 ML) RYE WHISKEY

★ ½ OZ (15 ML) SWEET VERMOUTH

★ ½ OZ (15 ML) YELLOW CHARTREUSE

★ 1 DASH ANGOSTURA BITTERS

★ 1 DASH ORANGE BITTERS

Pour all the ingredients into a mixing glass, add ice, and stir with a bar spoon.

Strain into a chilled cocktail glass.

GARNISH : squeeze a strip of lemon zest over the glass, and drop it in.

LOUISIANA COCKTAIL
Variation on Manhattan Cocktail

Here's a spirited take on the Manhattan, drawn from Stanley Clisby Arthur's Famous New Orleans Drinks & How to Mix 'Em, *dating from 1937.*

★ 1 OZ (25 ML) RYE WHISKEY
★ 1 OZ (25 ML) SWEET VERMOUTH
★ 1 OZ (25 ML) BÉNÉDICTINE
★ 2 DASHES PEYCHAUD'S BITTERS
★ 2 DASHES ABSINTHE

Pour all the ingredients into a mixing glass, add ice, and stir with a bar spoon.

Strain into a chilled cocktail glass.

GARNISH : add 1 maraschino cherry.

VIEUX CARRÉ
Variation on Manhattan Cocktail

Yet another response to the Manhattan hailing from the Big Easy, this drink was created in 1938 by Walter Bergeron.

★ 1 OZ (25 ML) RYE WHISKEY
★ 1 OZ (25 ML) SWEET VERMOUTH
★ 1 OZ (25 ML) COGNAC
★ 2 TSP (10 ML) BÉNÉDICTINE
★ 2 DASHES ANGOSTURA BITTERS
★ 2 DASHES PEYCHAUD'S BITTERS

Pour all the ingredients into a mixing glass, add ice, and stir with a bar spoon.

Strain into an ice-filled old-fashioned glass.

MARTINEZ COCKTAIL, 1862

The Martinez cocktail is seemingly the ancestor of the martini. We find the first mention of it made by Jerry Thomas in The Bar-Tender's Guide *of 1862.*

* 2 OZ (60 ML) SWEET VERMOUTH
* 1 OZ (25 ML) OLD TOM GIN
* 2 DASHES MARASCHINO LIQUEUR
* 1 DASH BOKER'S BITTERS

Pour all the ingredients into a mixing glass, add ice, and stir with a bar spoon.

Strain into a chilled cocktail glass.

GARNISH : squeeze a strip of lemon zest over the glass, and drop it in.

MARTINEZ COCKTAIL, MODERN RECIPE

Variation on Martinez Cocktail, 1862

* 1¾ OZ (50 ML) GIN
* 1 OZ (25 ML) SWEET VERMOUTH
* 2 TSP (10 ML) MARASCHINO LIQUEUR
* 2 DASHES ANGOSTURA BITTERS

Pour all the ingredients into a mixing glass, add ice, and stir with a bar spoon.

Strain into a chilled cocktail glass.

GARNISH : squeeze a strip of lemon zest over the glass, and drop it in.

OLD TOM GIN

Old Tom–style gin is sweeter than the London dry gin most familiar to us today. Adding sugar would let producers mask the inferior quality of certain gins in the eighteenth and nineteenth centuries, but it was also to the taste of that era's drinkers, who preferred a sweeter beverage.

MARTINEZ COCKTAIL, 1862

MINT JULEP

The mint julep is the signature drink of the South, dating from the beginning of the nineteenth century. It's classically prepared in a silver cup, which helps it stay chilled. Today, about 120,000 juleps are served each year at the Kentucky Derby. It's almost as great a feat as winning the horse race!

★ 10 MINT LEAVES
★ 2 TSP SUPERFINE SUGAR
★ 3 OZ (80 ML) BOURBON

In a julep cup, muddle the mint with the sugar.

Add the bourbon and fill the cup with crushed ice. Stir with a bar spoon. Add more crushed ice as needed.

GARNISH : crush 3 mint sprigs underneath the cup to release their flavor, then arrange them in a bouquet to garnish. Add a straw.

BOURBON

Bourbon is an American whiskey distilled from a minimum of 51 percent corn, generally rounded out with rye or wheat. It's mainly produced in the state of Kentucky, but more recently in other states, notably New York.

CHAMPAGNE JULEP

Variation on Mint Julep

This elaborate version of the julep was reported by Louis Fouquet in his Bariana, *published in 1896.*

- ⋆ 6 TO 8 MINT LEAVES, PLUS 1 SPRIG
- ⋆ 2 TSP SUPERFINE SUGAR
- ⋆ 1½ OZ (40 ML) VSOP COGNAC
- ⋆ 1 OZ (25 ML) YELLOW CHARTREUSE
- ⋆ CHAMPAGNE
- ⋆ JUICE OF ½ LEMON
- ⋆ SEASONAL FRUITS
- ⋆ 2 DASHES RHUM AGRICOLE VIEUX (AGED SUGARCANE RUM)

In a julep cup, muddle the mint leaves with 1 tsp of the sugar.

Add the cognac and fill the cup with crushed ice. Stir with a bar spoon, add the Chartreuse, and top off with champagne.

Dip the mint sprig in the lemon juice, then place it in the center of the cup. Garnish with seasonal fruits. Add the rum and sprinkle with the remaining 1 tsp sugar.

THE REAL GEORGIA MINT JULEP

Variation on Mint Julep

Here's a period piece from Jerry Thomas's The Bar-Tender's Guide, *published in 1862. Would they recognize it today down Georgia way?*

* MINT LEAVES
* 1 TSP SUPERFINE SUGAR
* 2 OZ (60 ML) VSOP COGNAC
* ¾ OZ (20 ML) CRÈME DE PÊCHE (PEACH LIQUEUR)

In a julep cup, muddle the mint with the sugar.

Add the cognac and the crème de pêche, then fill the cup with crushed ice. Stir with a bar spoon. Add more crushed ice as needed.

GARNISH : crush 3 mint sprigs underneath the cup to release their flavor, then arrange them in a bouquet to garnish. Add a straw.

MOSCOW MULE

MOSCOW MULE

The Moscow mule was born in 1940 in New York, but has always enjoyed more popularity on the West Coast. It was the brainchild of a meeting between John G. Martin, East Coast distributor of Smirnoff vodka, and Jack Morgan, proprietor of Cock 'n Bull brand ginger beer. Some say the name mule refers to the "kick" from the ginger beer. The Moscow mule is traditionally prepared in a copper mug.

★ 1¾ OZ (50 ML) RUSSIAN VODKA
★ 3½ OZ (100 ML) GINGER BEER
★ 1 OZ (25 ML) LIME JUICE

Pour all the ingredients into a mug or a highball glass, add ice, and stir with a bar spoon.

GARNISH : add lime rounds.

ELDERFLOWER GIN MULE
Variation on Moscow Mule (shaken cocktail)

★ 1¾ OZ (50 ML) GIN
★ ½ OZ (15 ML) ELDERFLOWER LIQUEUR
★ ½ OZ (15 ML) LIME JUICE
★ ½ OZ (15 ML) GRAPEFRUIT JUICE
★ 2 TSP (10 ML) LEMONGRASS SYRUP
★ 1 DASH PEYCHAUD'S BITTERS
★ 3½ OZ (100 ML) GINGER BEER

Pour all the ingredients except the ginger beer into a shaker, add ice, and shake vigorously.

Strain into an ice-filled highball glass. Top off with the ginger beer.

GARNISH : squeeze a strip of grapefruit zest over the glass, and garnish with a lemongrass stalk.

NEGRONI

The Negroni came onto the scene in 1919, at Florence's Casoni Café, when one Count Negroni was hankering after an aperitif that was a mite stronger than his usual Americano. So he asked barman Fosco Scarelli to replace the fizzy water with gin. The concoction quickly grew in popularity and, of course, they called it the Negroni.

* 1½ OZ (40 ML) GIN
* 1 OZ (25 ML) CAMPARI
* ¾ OZ (20 ML) SWEET VERMOUTH

Pour all the ingredients into a mixing glass, add ice, and stir with a bar spoon.

Strain into an ice-filled old-fashioned glass.

GARNISH : squeeze a strip of orange zest over the glass, and drop it in.

NEGRONI SBAGLIATO

"Incorrect" Negroni

* 1 OZ (25 ML) SWEET VERMOUTH
* 1 OZ (25 ML) CAMPARI
* 2 OZ (60 ML) SPUMANTE OR CHAMPAGNE

Pour all the ingredients into an old-fashioned glass, add an ice cube, and stir with a bar spoon.

GARNISH : squeeze a strip of orange zest over the glass, and drop it in.

BOULEVARDIER

Variation on Negroni

Here is another play on the Negroni, created in 1927 at Harry's New York Bar in Paris by founder and proprietor Harry MacElhone himself.

✳ 1½ OZ (40 ML) BOURBON
✳ 1 OZ (25 ML) SWEET VERMOUTH
✳ 1 OZ (25 ML) CAMPARI

Pour all the ingredients into a mixing glass, add ice, and stir with a bar spoon.

Strain into an ice-filled old-fashioned glass.

GARNISH : squeeze a strip of orange zest over the glass, and drop it in.

AGAVE NEGRONI

Variation on Negroni

✳ 1½ OZ (40 ML) WHITE TEQUILA (100% AGAVE)
✳ 1 OZ (25 ML) CAMPARI
✳ ¾ OZ (20 ML) ITALIAN VERMOUTH
✳ 1 DASH ORANGE BITTERS

Pour all the ingredients into a mixing glass, add ice, and stir with a bar spoon.

Strain into an old-fashioned glass and add an ice cube.

NEGRONI

OLD FASHIONED

Behold the ur-cocktail: spirit, sugar, and aromatic bitters (see History, page 10). The preparation of the old fashioned is, naturally, subject to controversy. Some prefer to dissolve a bitters-soaked sugar cube and prepare the cocktail directly in the glass, adding progressively more bourbon and ice while stirring with a bar spoon. Others appreciate a smoother texture and use sugar syrup. You can vary this recipe by replacing the bourbon with another spirit like rum, tequila, or even gin.

✶ 1 TSP (5 ML) SUGAR SYRUP
✶ 1 TSP (5 ML) SPARKLING WATER
✶ 2 DASHES ANGOSTURA BITTERS
✶ ORANGE ZEST
✶ 2 OZ (60 ML) BOURBON

Combine the sugar syrup, sparkling water, bitters, and orange zest in a mixing glass. Lightly muddle the zest to extract its essential oils.

Take out the zest, then add the bourbon and ice. Stir with a bar spoon and strain into an ice-filled old-fashioned glass.

GARNISH : squeeze a strip of orange zest over the glass, and drop it in.

RED SNAPPER

The red snapper is a derivation of the better-known bloody Mary. The story goes that a barman who earned his stripes at Harry's New York Bar in Paris later emigrated to New York and modified the bloody Mary recipe, created at Harry's Bar in the 1920s, by replacing the vodka—less popular at the time in the United States—with gin. There are quite a few variations on the bloody Mary: you can vary the seasonings and play with the flavors; try soy sauce, cilantro, cucumber, or spicy red chiles.

* 1½ OZ (40 ML) GIN
* 3½ OZ (100 ML) TOMATO JUICE
* 2 TSP (10 ML) LEMON JUICE
* 2 TSP (10 ML) WORCESTERSHIRE SAUCE
* 1 TSP CELERY SALT
* 5 DROPS OF TABASCO
* 1 GRINDING BLACK PEPPER

Pour all the ingredients into a mixing glass, add ice, and stir with a bar spoon.

Strain into a highball glass with several ice cubes.

GARNISH : add 1 celery stick and 1 lemon round or strip of lemon zest.

SAZERAC

The Sazerac traces its origin to New Orleans, where it was invented by a Creole apothecary by the name of Antoine Amédée Peychaud, in 1830. Peychaud's bitters are a brand of aromatic bitters created by this same Peychaud, and still on the market today.

* 2 OZ (60 ML) RYE WHISKEY OR COGNAC
* 1 TSP (5 ML) SUGAR SYRUP
* 3 DASHES PEYCHAUD'S BITTERS
* 1 DASH ANGOSTURA BITTERS
* 1 DASH ABSINTHE

Pour all the ingredients except the absinthe into a mixing glass, add ice, and stir with a bar spoon.

Pour the absinthe into a chilled old-fashioned glass, swirl the glass to coat the sides with the liqueur, then pour out the excess. Strain the contents of the mixing glass into the absinthe-rinsed glass.

GARNISH : squeeze a strip of lemon zest over the glass.

TOM COLLINS

This recipe is drawn from Jerry Thomas's The Bar-Tender's Guide, *published in 1862.*

* 1¾ OZ (50 ML) GIN
* 1 OZ (25 ML) LEMON JUICE
* ½ OZ (15 ML) SUGAR SYRUP
* SPARKLING WATER

Pour all the ingredients except the sparkling water into a highball glass, add ice, and stir with a bar spoon. Top off with sparkling water.

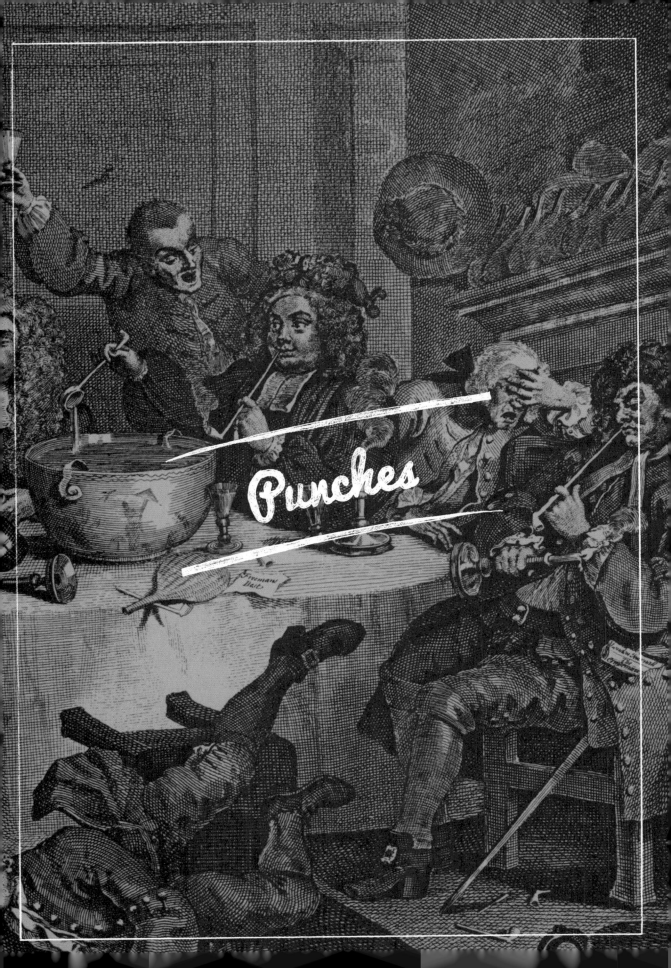

Punches

HOT GIN PUNCH

This punch is adapted from a recipe of Charles Dickens's, dating from around 1850. For this punch, it's important to not let the mixture come to a boil. On the other hand, the longer the punch is cooked, the more the flavors will concentrate and the amount of alcohol will decrease. Sip this one by the fireside.

* 3 TBSP HONEY
* ¾ CUP (6 OZ/180 ML) HOT WATER
* 2 CUPS (16 OZ/500 ML) GIN
* 2 CUPS (16 OZ/500 ML) MADEIRA WINE
* ¾ CUP (6 OZ/180 ML) LEMON JUICE
* 2 TSP RAW SUGAR
* 2 TSP GROUND CINNAMON
* 4 LEMON SLICES STUDDED WITH CLOVES
* 2 ORANGE SLICES
* 4 CHUNKS PINEAPPLE
* 1 PINCH GRATED NUTMEG

In a pot, dissolve the honey in the hot water.

Add all the remaining ingredients and heat over low heat.

Serve ladled into warm teacups.

GARNISH : add 1 cinnamon stick and 1 lemon round studded with cloves.

PHILADELPHIA FISH HOUSE PUNCH

This 1795 recipe was a specialty of Philadelphia's "State in Schuylkill," also known as the "Fish House." Founded in 1732, it was the first fishing club in U.S. history, a place where Colonial notables would slip their domestic tethers and enjoy cigars, whiskey, and punch. This punch is traditionally prepared over a block of ice, but you can use ice cubes.

⋆ 2 PARTS DARK JAMAICAN RUM

⋆ 1 PART COGNAC

⋆ ½ PART PEACH BRANDY OR CRÈME DE PÊCHE (PEACH LIQUEUR)

⋆ 1 PART LEMON JUICE

⋆ 1 PART SIMPLE SYRUP

⋆ 2 PARTS MINERAL WATER OR COLD BLACK TEA

Pour all the ingredients into a punch bowl.

Add a block of ice and serve at once.

GARNISH : add lemon rounds and seasonal fruits.

PUNCH À LA SOYER

We owe this recipe to Alexis Benoît Soyer, a French chef who emigrated to London and became very popular during the first half of the nineteenth century. He was one of London's cocktail pioneers.

✶ 2 PARTS GIN
✶ 1 PART MARASCHINO LIQUEUR
✶ 1 PART LEMON JUICE
✶ 2 PARTS SPARKLING WATER

Pour all the ingredients into a punch bowl.

Add a block of ice and serve chilled.

GARNISH : add lemon rounds or zest.

RUSSIAN SPRING PUNCH

This punch was created in London by Dick Bradsell, in the 1990s.

- ✶ 1 PART RUSSIAN VODKA
- ✶ 1 PART LEMON JUICE
- ✶ ⅓ PART SUGAR SYRUP
- ✶ 2 PARTS CHAMPAGNE
- ✶ ½ PART CRÈME DE CASSIS
  (BLACK CURRANT LIQUEUR)

Pour the vodka, lemon juice, and sugar syrup into an ice-filled highball glass.

Stir with a bar spoon.

Top off with the champagne and, lastly, the crème de cassis.

GARNISH : add 1 lemon slice.

THE GREEN BEAST

When absinthe came back on the scene in the 2000s, many drinkers were intrigued but uncertain as to what to do with it. This punch gave them a clue— it was created by French bartender Charles Vexenat for Pernod Absinthe.

⋆ 1 PART ABSINTHE
⋆ 1 PART LIME JUICE
⋆ 1 PART SIMPLE SYRUP
⋆ 4 PARTS MINERAL WATER
⋆ SLICED CUCUMBER

Pour all the liquid ingredients into a punch bowl.

Add a block of ice and the cucumber slices.

Serve chilled.

VOIRON SUMMER PUNCH

I created this punch as an homage to the birthplace of Chartreuse.

* 2 PARTS GIN
* 1 PART LIME JUICE
* ½ PART YELLOW CHARTREUSE
* ½ PART SIMPLE SYRUP
* 2 PARTS MINERAL WATER
* A FEW DASHES ORANGE BITTERS, DEPENDING ON TOTAL VOLUME

Pour all the ingredients into a punch bowl.

Add a block of ice and serve chilled.

GARNISH : add lemon and lime rounds or zest and seasonal fruits.

INGREDIENT INDEX

BIBLIOGRAPHY

CRADDOCK (Harry), *The Savoy Cocktail Book*, Pavilion Books Ltd, 1930.

ENSSLIN (Hugo R.), *Recipes for Mixed Drinks*, New York, Fox Printing House, 1916.

FOUQUET (Louis), *Bariana,* Jared Brown, 1896.

JOHNSON (Harry), *New and Improved Bartender's Manual*, Createspace, 1882.

TARLING (William J.), *Cafe Royal Cocktail Book*, Mixellany Books, 1937.

THOMAS (Jerry), *The Bar-Tender's Guide or How to Mix Drinks*, New York, Dick and Fitzgerald Publishers, 1862.

WONDRICH (David), *Punch: The Delights (and Dangers) of the Flowing Bowl*, Penguin Group USA, 2010.

Credits

Illustrations : pp. 122-123 : Hogarth, William 1697–1764,
A Modern Midnight Conversation, c. 1765.
Engravings : pp. 10, 13, 29, 35, 41, 51, 80, 104 : Pepin Press;
pp. 10, 56, 72 : *Victorian Goods and Merchandise,* Dover Publications, Inc.

ACKNOWLEDGMENTS

Thanks to Coralie Ferreira, Claire Guigal,
Juliette Spiteri, and Virginie Garnier for
their professionalism and their good
humor. Thanks to Jonathan Sellam,
Thomas Kolnikoff, and all the staff of
La Maison Mère restaurant for their
kind welcome. Thanks to Clémence
Charpentier, Éric Fossard, Laurence
Marrot, and Thierry Daniel for their help.
Thanks to Fanny for her patience.
Thanks to Nadine Ziadé Postel for the
meeting. Thanks to my family and
my friends for their support.

Weldon Owen is a division of Bonnier Corporation
1045 Sansome Street, Suite 100, San Francisco, CA 94111
www.weldonowen.com

Library of Congress Cataloging-in-Publication data is available

This edition printed in 2015
10 9 8 7 6 5 4 3 2 1

ISBN 13: 978-1-61628-960-7
ISBN 10: 1-61628-960-0

Printed in China by Toppan Leefung Printing Limited